Lady Bracknell's Confinement
or, The Bunburyist

A monologue

Paul Doust

Samuel French—London
New York-Toronto-Hollywood

CHARACTERS

Lady Bracknell

Voices off stage:
Jack
Gwendolen
Chasuble
Miss Prism
Algernon

The action takes place in the hall of the manor house, Woolton, Hertfordshire

Time —a July afternoon in 1895, shortly after tea

LADY BRACKNELL'S CONFINEMENT
or, THE BUNBURYIST

The hall of the manor house, Hertfordshire. A July afternoon in 1895, shortly after tea

The hall contains at least one piece of furniture on which a person might sit. There is also a tall pedestal on which stands a grotesquely ornate vase of the most beautiful, pure-white lilies

From the morning-room, off, the following dialogue is heard

Jack M. Generals ... Mallam, Maxbohm, Magley — what ghastly names they have — Markby, Migsby, Mobbs, Moncrieff! Lieutenant eighteen forty, Captain, Lieutenant-Colonel, Colonel, General eighteen sixty-nine, Christian names, Ernest John. I always told you, Gwendolen, my name was Ernest, didn't I? Well, it is Ernest after all. I mean it naturally is Ernest.

Lady Bracknell Yes, I remember now that the General was called Ernest. I knew I had some particular reason for disliking the name.

Gwendolen Ernest! My own Ernest! I felt from the first that you could have no other name!

Jack Gwendolen, it is a terrible thing for a man to find out suddenly that all his life he has been speaking nothing but the truth. Can you forgive me?

Gwendolen I can. For I feel that you are sure to change.

Jack My own one!

Dr Chasuble Laetitia!

Miss Prism Frederick! At last!

Algernon Cecily! At last!

Jack Gwendolen! At last!

Lady Bracknell My nephew, you seem to be displaying signs of triviality.

Jack On the contrary, Aunt Augusta, I've now realized for the the first time in my life the vital Importance of Being Earnest.

Lady Bracknell enters from the morning-room. Pause

Lady Bracknell A hand-bag? (*Pause*) The coincidence is remarkable!

Silence

I am very much afraid that the news I have to give Mr Worthing will not altogether please him. It has been my misfortune to witness, only moments ago, an embrace of some passion involving my daughter, Gwendolen, and the gentleman in question. I cannot possibly allow such an indecorous intersection to maintain itself. I rarely undeceive people; it is not part of my system. In this instance, however, the felicity of my daughter's future is at stake and I feel it my duty to act.

Pause

Mr Worthing is the son of my poor sister, Mrs Moncrieff, and consequently Gwendolen's elder brother. But whilst Gwendolen is indeed my daughter I, alas, am not her mother. I am, however, her father.

Silence

I was born both in eighteen forty-six and in Stepney. My parents, both of whom were members of the working classes, christened me "William Gallfin". My mother was a sail-maker, my father a dock-labourer both were revolutionaries. In her few, but dangerously industrious, leisure hours my mother had devised an exercise program for her female peers, entitled: "Physical Pulchritude for the Working Woman." My father, however, was a radical nonconformist and consequently posed a less immediate threat to the order of society. Neither parent, I am delighted to report, lived to exert the full force of their misguided ideals. The Great Cholera Pandemic of eighteen forty-nine sapped my mother of her pulchritude within a week and her life inside a fortnight. And on my fourteenth birthday my father was hit on the head by a flying projectile whilst on a Chartist march to the House of Lords. It later transpired that the projectile was, itself, the charter which, having been signed by some three thousand two hundred and sixty-five dock-labourers of Wapping, weighed a full fifty pounds and struck him dead on impact. A fitting demise, I think, for a radical nonconformist.

In life I have rarely entertained affection. My principal adhesions have always been to monetary gain and social regard, and those who do not share my enthusiasms are quite beyond my understanding. This is due, I think, to the single act of intelligence of which my parents were capable. Both mother and father remained utterly insensible to my existence throughout the entirety of my childhood. For this I am most grateful. To love is to care and to care is to be weak. Indifference is the fortress of the wise. To love, even a little, is to enter the valley of the fool.

With the happy termination of my parents I found myself liberated into loneliness. For some time I had harboured an affinity with the Drama and now, though my means were small, contrived that a visit to the theatre became, for me, a regular escape from the morbidity of my daily existence. In the Garden of the Theatre the seeds of Reality fall on barren ground only to wither in the shade of fruitful Fantasy and Delusion. This is, of course, quite as it should be. To cultivate delusion is to take the first real step towards a permanent dislocation from reality, and a marked dislocation from reality is fundamental to robust mental health. Of this I am quite convinced and I have often attempted to communicate its truth to poor Lord Bracknell. He, however, believing it his duty to make some sense of the world and its machinations lies, at this very moment, in a darkened room where he is gripped by both sanity and a straight-jacket.

It came to my attention that the Lyceum theatre was to present *Orpheus and his Lyre*. This classical romance was an unrelentingly complicated piece and additional labour was to be procured for its production. I volunteered my services at once and found myself in the employ of Miss Betty Bridley; a declamatory actress of fluctuating age and shape. The actress was to give her Eurydice; I was to give my assistance. My chief function was to engineer Miss Bridley's many and diverse sartorial transmogrifications; but my secondary responsibility lay in assisting her with the memorization of her role, and in this task I took my greatest pleasure. Indeed, I recall many happy hours hearing Miss Bridley's pauses.

Before any public performance of her art Miss Bridley would execute ritual-like preparations. These preparations included the flooding of her throat with an unsavoury brew which she kept at a constant temperature by means of a bi-metallic receptacle perilously suspended above a Bunsen burner. This apparatus stood on her dressing-room table and next to it a large porcelain bowl of dark volatile pulp. This pulp seemed principally composed of rotting vegetable matter and it's claims to youth-giving properties explained, I think, the frenzy of desperation with which the actress applied it to her face.

One inglorious evening, an evening of irrevocable consequence for both the actress and myself, Miss Bridley made a calamitous error. In a moment of mental abberation she applied the Bunsened brew to her brow whilst simultaneously swallowing the vegetable compost. In so doing the actress robbed herself of both voice and feature in one disastrous act of negligence. On opening her mouth to speak the previously vociferous Miss Bridley was now able to produce only the lifeless squeak of insensible salad. Upon referring her face to the looking-glass she plunged instantly into a coma. As Miss Bridley lay at my feet, now mercifully oblivious to her condition, I marvelled at the vindictiveness of a concoction which had disarranged her once delicately contoured profile into an outline now more akin to the hastily executed work of a lesser French impressionist.

There was nothing to be done. From my many hours of work with Miss Bridley I knew the role of Eurydice to be quite beyond the recollective powers of a lesser thespian, so with the collapse of the actress I naturally expected a similarly incapacitating effect upon the production. I had not, however, anticipated the vigorous intercession of the stage manager.

"William, my boy...", he drawled, "...you must play the part."

My coiffure assumed instant perpendicularity.

"Me, sir? What has it to do with me, sir?"

"It's a fatter-complete ...", he continued, "... and no messing. You know the words better than any other bugger and you're still young enough to pass as a girl. Don't worry, my old china, I'll break it to the gang; you just look lively and strap y' gubbins into them Grecian folds."

To comprehend my eventual complicity in this scheme it is important to understand the exact nature of my existence at that time and its complete antipathy to my innate gentlemanly aspirations. I earned my living in the theatre whilst residing in a singular hovel below a fishmonger's in Pimlico. Were I to accept the stage manager's proposal, I reasoned, the financial reward promised me would surely be sufficient to enable my first step on to the ladder of society? This achieved I would cast off the motley forever and, dragging myself bodily out of the quagmire, begin my ascent with vigour!

With only a few minor alterations I found that Miss Bridley's costumes fitted me with a bewildering accuracy. Indeed, once furnished about in womanly attire my sex became quite indiscernible. Light-fingered Time has since pilfered away the more ornamental trinkets of my youth, but I think it not impermissible to claim that, as a girl, Beauty was my closest ally.

I am told, incidentally, that Miss Bridley has proved most resourceful with regard to her facial misfortune, having secured a degree of acceptance for her now singular aspect by moving to Stoke Poges and opening an arts and crafts shop.

One night, following a performance, there came a dull knock at my dressing-room door. Whilst psychologically I had thrown of my stage persona sartorially I had not. But I had no time to deny my caller entry before the door was thrown open and he had presented himself to me. This was my first encounter with the man who was to marry me and go mad.

Poor Lord Bracknell is now sadly bereft of all cognitive faculty and whilst I concede that this is, in part, the result of his union with myself I do not consider it entirely of my own doing. The canker of mental entropy was evident even then. He bore a small grouping of strangulated flowers which he foisted in my direction with his Neanderthal fist. Though astonished at the creature's credulity I thought it neither fair nor necessary to undeceive him as to my sex. I accepted his bouquet and awaited his departure. He did not, however, go away but continued merely to hover.

"Is there anything else, Mr Fairfax?"

He had introduced himself as Gerald Fairfax and it was some time before I was to learn of the title he was to inherit.

"Er ... I'm to give a t-tea party at my home next week. T-tea, cucumber sandwiches, that sort of that thing. And ... well ... I'd be so delight-t-ted if you could at-t-tend. May I please leave you an invit-t-tation?" He did so and, at last, departed.

That night, below the fishmonger's, I looked, and looked again, at the invitation. The curiosity of his cravat had intimated Gerald's nobleness of birth but the address on the invitation confirmed the giddy heights of his subsequent attainment. Number one-o-four Upper Grosvenor Square — the fashionable side! It was impossible, of course, that I should accept his invitation. Mr Fairfax had approached a young lady and so he would hardly be gratified at the appearance of a young man. Yet would it be so very wrong to taste, just once, the fruits of privilege? To dine at the table of plenty and sup on the honey-dew of social esteem? Be it only a tea party ... If I might know, however fleetingly, the delights of refinement I could surely endure with repose an eternity of degradation.

I found little difficulty in dressing for my adventure since Miss Bridley's wardrobe was only marginally less extensive than the woman herself. I arrived at Gerald's in good time and complete confidence. This was largely due to the speed of my carriage and the elegance of a bonnet perfectly constructed by Edith, a bewilderingly eccentric young milliner in my employ.

Tea at Gerald's was an easily executed triumph since most of those present were visibly devoted to Mr William Morris and therefore quite prone to deception. My theatrical experience, too, was of great assistance to me. In the theatre one is compelled to learn words and gestures with which one is entirely unfamiliar and to employ them with decision without once reflecting upon what they might actually mean. This facility, I soon realized, commanded a great respect amongst the educated classes, and it won me invitations to all the nobler households of London — including, indeed, that of Mary Farquhar, a woman of little background and almost no perception and who has consequently become so dear a friend. These invitations were invariably addressed to "The Friend of Mr Fairfax", as I had become so charmingly nomenclatured. I had explained to Gerald that my off-stage identity must, of necessity, remain a secret to both him and to society at large. When he pressed me for an explanation I answered only with a smile. This smile had taken me many months to perfect and succeeded in proving sufficiently Sphinx-like to maintain his interest whilst revealing absolutely nothing. This smile has served me well now for many years, and I hold it as one of my more useful facial distortions. Indeed, I count this smile as one of the very few valuable acquisitions I made at the fishmonger's where I copied it from the face of a more than usually deceitful smoked haddock.

It soon became clear to me, however, that this smile alone could not be expected to cover every eventuality. The Friend of Mr Fairfax, though lionized by society, had, of necessity, to perish. Her death was vital to the well-being of William Gallfin. But how to achieve it? An incapacitating collision with a Salvationist's tambourine had suggested itself as the most fitting and instantaneous mode of expiry, and even now I cannot hear, "Onward Christian Soldiers" without a momentary suicidal impulse. But that moment was lost many years ago and "Lady Bracknell" goes marching on. At the tea party I had tasted the confection of nobility and had found it rare, digestible and fatally addictive.

Gerald's association with myself afforded him a confidence he might otherwise never have known and when he finally declared his love for me it came as little surprise, still less his proposal of marriage. I had equipped myself entirely for this eventuality, devising a mono-syllabic refusal that even Gerald's

retarded understanding might grapple with: "No". But this
refusal was never to be delivered for a quite unexpected
ingredient in Gerald's proposal threw my decision into complete disarray.

"A title"! That is what he had said. "A title"!

Gerald was imminently to inherit a title and if he were to
become a lord then I, if married to him, would inevitably
become a lady!

"Lady Bracknell"! The phrase gyrated in my cranium with
giddying effect."Lady Bracknell"!

I begged time to reflect upon Gerald's proposal. In actuality I
desired, for a short while at least, to savour the fantasy before
disposing of it forever. It was while thus engaged that I
received a letter. It's contents were as brief as they were
alarming;

> "Dear Friend of Mr Fairfax,
> I know your secret. Call on me.
> Augusta Leclercq."

Mary Farquhar could tell me but little of the Leclercqs. The
family, though highly esteemed, had not been active in society
for some while. Augusta and her younger sister, Caroline,
lived a sadly circumscribed existence due to the proximity of
an aging but indomitable mother. The Leclercqs' residence, so
Mary told me, was large, fashionable, but remote. I made my
way to Belgravia.

It was a sun-bright afternoon when I visited the Leclercqs,
although the dim recesses of the parlour in which I waited
prevented the discernment of any such meteorological gaiety.
A variety of paintings adorned the walls and I was pleased to
find not a hint of modernism in the entire assemblage. I was

astounded, however, into an audible gasp as my eyes alighted upon a portrait above the fireplace. The woman in the picture might have been myself so closely did she resemble my every feature. Our crinolines were of a different hue — and mine perhaps a little more in step with fashion — but this disparity apart the verisimilitude of our facial geography was remarkable, and not a little disquieting. Her eyes were my eyes, her chin my chin, and, as I looked more closely still, I felt sure I perceived upon her lips something of the smile so often associated with myself.

"Yes", came a voice from behind me, "I, too, am a student of haddock."

I turned. Standing before me was Augusta Leclercq. The similarity expounded by the artist was as nothing to that achieved by nature.

"Won't you take tea?", entreated my reflection.

It transpired that although incarcerated within the house by maternal vigilance, Miss Leclercq obtained information of the outer world by way of her trusty and loquacious maid, Gloria. It was through this irreverent channel that Miss Leclercq had first learnt of, "The Mysterious One", as Gloria had so melo-dramatically referred to me. It seemed that on an errand for her mistress, Gloria had had occasion to visit the very fish-monger's below which I dwelt. From this vantage point the maid had observed "The Mysterious One" stealing out of the basement door. She had then procured from the proprietor, by means which can only be guessed at for no coinage was exchanged, the exact nature of my actual identity together with a pound of jellied eels.

I am glad to report that Gloria is no longer with us, having totally died of a rare water-borne botulism. This is both fitting and fortunate. Had the activities of such a servant been allowed to continue they would certainly have proved the undoing of the entire British aristocracy, not to mention the bankrupting of the Billingsgate Market.

Miss Leclercq had now concluded her revelations and I awaited her threat of blackmail with as much equanimity as I could muster. But such a threat was not forthcoming. Instead Miss Leclercq merely poured more tea and explained that we were,

"... ideally suited to a reciprocal arrangement of benefit to us both...", and won't I please call her Augusta?

It seemed that Augusta's younger sister, Caroline, longed for matrimony. Their mother's doctrines, however, forbade Caroline's marriage until a suitable union had been effected for Augusta; and herein lay the difficulty. For, although concerned for her sister's happiness, Augusta was as passionate in her abhorrence of the married state as Caroline was desirous of it. Augusta offered no explanation for her unnatural attitude beyond a radical interpretation of the life and work of Miss Vesta Tilly.

"Could we not ...", continued Augusta, "... execute the exchange of identities which our physical similarity has already made so very possible?"

I was astounded; and still more so when Augusta declared knowledge of Gerald's proposal to me. This marriage, she suggested, would be my reward in the enterprise; hers would be a liberation into the world beyond Belgravia and the freedom to pursue a variety of revolutionary activities.

My mind spun at the possibilities now presented to me. The Leclercqs, by Mary Farquhar's own admission, were a highly respected family. To lead them back into society, by way of nuptial union with the family Fairfax, would be a delight to London and a considerable achievement for myself. Gone would be the need for any shilly-shallying as to my parentage. Here was an impeccable ancestry that I might acquire complete. Here was the road to "Lady Bracknell"!

There remained, it seemed, only one question. Quite simply: could it be done? Would not Augusta's family recognize an imposter at once and demand the immediate reinstatement of the original? Here, explained Augusta, infirmity of the optical kind was our ally. Her sister Caroline was severely limited visually by a remarkable shortsightedness, dutifully developed out of a great respect for modern art. And the mother, on her eleventh birthday, had closed her eyes and had refused ever to open them again. This was due, I later gathered, to a grotesquely irreligious encounter with an ostentatious cleric.

So it was that my metamorphosis was contrived. By the end of that clandestine afternoon "William Gallfin" had been laid to rest and "Augusta Leclercq" had taken complete and magnificent occupation!

There was, of course, one other question which I might have found it timely to address: "What on earth am I doing?" But this question I chose to ignore; for my wit had been addled by Ambition and the worm of Avarice dwelt in my heart.

I am pleased to report that the real Augusta's influence on the world has so far proved minimal. She now resides, as far as I am aware, deep in the Americas where she manufactures small plaster paperweights cast in the form of "The Helmet of Athene". But I do not allow this to trouble my conscience.

It was a quite simple matter to convince Gerald that I had all the while been the daughter of a fine family and that, should he still wish to marry me, I would be delighted to abandon the theatre and become his wife. Gerald's simple mind accepted

my story without question and I left it to him to communicate
our marital intentions to society at large. This he did with the
speed of Mercury and, following my happy introduction to his
family, we were married. A little while later Caroline, my
newly acquired sister, was herself united with a personage of
military persuasions, male, and our full happiness was finally
attained when our mother, very thoughtfully, died.

The name of Caroline's husband was Colonel Ernest John
Moncrieff and their union was soon fruitful. A son was born
to the couple whom they christened, naturally enough, Ernest.
The child was a joy to us all; with the notable exception of my
husband. The adhesion I had to Gerald was, inevitably, barren.
Not that he had ever been made to suffer conjugal deprivations
of any kind; far from it. Throughout the early years of our
marriage I contrived to execute my matrimonial obligations
by means of an elaborate deception which poor Lord Bracknell's
limited intelligence has never uncovered, and which my own
gentility will not allow me to describe. It was at about this
time, however, that Gerald fell into the first of his recurring
and ever more debilitating spells of melancholia and I cannot
help but conclude that this was, in some measure, the result of
our own childless state.

But any husband is a volatile attachment. Indeed, it is a sorry
fact that the man who is an ornament to society when single
may, when married, become a hideous carbuncle to his wife.
Such was the nature of Caroline's husband. The ignominies
my poor sister was forced to endure were many and extreme,
and on more than one occasion she sought solace in the relative
tranquillity of my own home. It was on just such an occasion
as this that the first in a series of remarkable calamities
occurred.

When visiting me Caroline, and the infant Ernest, would
invariably be accompanied by the child's governess, Miss
Prism. On the day in question Prism had taken the baby out in

its perambulator. She had with her a hand-bag in which she intended to place a manuscript of a work of fiction which she had bludgeoned together in her moments of idleness. Prism never returned. A few weeks later the perambulator was discovered at midnight standing by itself in a remote corner of Bayswater. It contained the manuscript of a three-volumed novel of more than usually revolting sentimentality. But the baby was not there. It is only now, many years later, that an explanation, as horrible as it is unlikely, has provided itself.

In a moment of unforgivable indifference Prism had deposited the manuscript in the bassinette and placed the baby in the hand-bag. She then left the hand-bag in the cloak-room of one of the larger railway stations of London. Victoria. The Brighton Line. The hand-bag, it seems, was then found by the late Mr Thomas Cardew. The child was given the name "Worthing", an appellation inspired by the fact that the said Mr Cardew happened to be journeying towards Worthing at the time. Worthing, as I know only too well, is a place in Sussex. It comprises a tram-line, a pebble and an insipid breeze. Nobody lives there, although I know it to be reasonably well populated.

Before his death Mr Cardew and a further hand-bag were to enter my life with a coincidence I now see to be both remarkable and excessively distressing.

The disappearance of her son left Caroline quite inconsolable and it is indicative of the tone of their relationship that she bore her husband no further children for a full four years following the incident. The birth of their second son, Algernon, was augmented almost immediately by the death of his father. One must take care with colonic irrigation.

Caroline now found herself alone and penniless, for on his death the General was revealed to be both remarkably stupid and devastatingly bankrupt, having lost his considerable family fortune as the result of a characteristically reckless game of dominoes with a suspiciously numerate Bengal Lancer.

With the ever-increasing demands of a small child, coupled to severe financial difficulties, Caroline once again turned to her sister and it was not long before both she and Algernon had taken residence under my roof.

Caroline's wounds began gradually to heal, her nimbleness of spirit to return and the extraordinary bloom of her particular beauty to re-establish itself. My sister, I now saw for the first time, was, indeed, a creature of wonder and I was not at all surprised when, little more than a year since she had been resident at Grosvenor Square, a letter arrived for her. Caroline read me the letter, as was her custom with all such correspondence:

> "Dear Mrs Moncrieff,
> You are beautiful and I love you. May we meet?
> Yours, William."

Caroline seemed quite unable to comprehend its meaning. I explained, "Why, don't you see my dear? This William, whoever he might be, desires your further acquaintance. Have you not read the additional note at the bottom of the letter?"

> "NB I shall call this Sunday afternoon at half-past four. Hope and pray that you will be at home."

By a remarkable coincidence I was to be in the country that very weekend. This, as I explained to Caroline, would allow her a certain privacy with which to entertain "The Mysterious One", as I referred to him.

I returned, as promised, on the Monday morning. How I longed to hear Caroline's report of her meeting with William.

The gentleman in question, it is important to understand, was almost as much a stranger to myself as he was to my sister, and I could not possibly allow their further acquaintance until satisfied that Caroline had found their initial encounter a happy one. I saw no reason to doubt this.

Her words, I felt sure, would be a delight to me. She would speak of a high and kindly gentleman. A gentleman whose cloudy heart had adored her for so long and from so very near at hand, but whose feet of clay forbade him to approach her until now. She would describe his tender yet distant manner. She would repeat the pale and whispered words which had stumbled from his mouth, giving voice to his terrible and passionate admiration, as dark and as secret the hyacinth, yet speaking only silence of himself. She would lament the enforced brevity of their meeting, weep for the dusty sorrow of his departure, but exult in the remembered joy of their momentary union, of the Pleasure That Aabideth for a Moment. Assuredly, she would describe love?

Pause

But Caroline did not, that day, speak to me of the meeting. Indeed, it was some months before she found the need to confide in me at all. When she did so it was in an agony of desperation. She spat of a brute and barbarian monster who had snatched her in his grasp and torn her savagely in two leaving her spiritually broken, bodily degraded — and alone. Alone in the Sorrow That Endureth Forever. And her beautiful eyes filled with tears.

Pause

Shocked as I was, I comforted poor Caroline as every really affectionate sister must. I assured her that any creature possessed of so foul a soul had no place in her heart and was best left to fester in the disgusting ugliness of his own.

Pause

On this point I was more than usually confident.

Silence

It was clear to me that Caroline, widowed as she was, could not possibly be exposed to the scrutiny of the world whilst carrying a child. Indeed, the birth of any such infant seemed quite out of the question. Yet Caroline longed for the baby; and I, myself, was not entirely indifferent to its birth. I devised, therefore, a scheme. The child would, in actuality, be born to Caroline whilst in the eyes of the world it would be the produce of Lady Bracknell. We agreed the idea and began our plans in ernest.

Caroline should depart, at once, to a place entirely bereft of intelligent population. We chose, therefore, the town of Worthing. With my sister thus safely ensconced I announced to Lord Bracknell that his hopes had fructified and that he was to become a father. He seemed suitably delighted as far as I could discern. I then set about simulating the distortions of body evidenced in women by the progenitorial process and retired into a confinement of my own.

I achieved the necessary effect by means of a robust rubber balloon securely concealed beneath my petticoats. This balloon could be inflated progressively until the actual infant became available. Although this deception proved ultimately successful, its execution was not as simple as I had originally conceived. On more than one occasion the rubber sphere disobligingly released a little of its air, thus making a rude declaration of its existence. Such noises I could usually pass of as the eructive consequence of a prolonged confinement. There was one occasion, however, when a more than usually volcanic blast caught me entirely unawares, ripping the laces from my boots and hurling me bodily across the room at a velocity previously equaled only by Stephenson's Rocket.

The months passed. Toward the end of my confinement I found myself entirely alone in the house — apart, that is, from the gibbering but indistinct presence of poor Lord Bracknell — due to the fact that I had temporarily dismissed all the servants in order to facilitate Caroline's undetected return. My husband's increased sensibility, I feel bound to explain, was principally due to the imminent realization of his fatherhood. Indeed, so impressed was Lord Bracknell by my somewhat sudden fecundity that he was, in the end, to demand a second child of me. This I produced, some years latter, in the form of Gerald junior; a child of the male sex whom I procured, by means of a small coin, at the saloon-bar of a more than usually dissolute gin-palace on the Old Kent Road. But this extraordinariness of origin was as nothing compared to the circumstances surrounding the arrival of our first child.

I had not heard from Caroline for some while and as her time was now near, my anxiety was naturally extreme. One morning, having risen unusually early in order to mend a puncture, I heard a timid knocking at my front door. I realized instantly that this would be Caroline who, with the newborn child, had stolen up from the coast at dawn in order to avoid discovery. I hurried downstairs — threw open the door! But neither Caroline nor, indeed, any human being were there. On the step, however, sat a vulgarly new and elaborately reinforced hand-bag, and next to it an envelope of provincial quality.

I retreated, with both hand-bag and envelope, to the privacy of my bedroom. I opened the letter.

"Dear Madam,
Please excuse this mode of delivery but I am relatively unschooled in these matters. The single previous experience of this nature which I have had involved a hand-bag of this kind and I merely follow precedent.

"I am a sometime-resident of one of the smaller seaside resorts of Sussex. Yesterday, whilst taking my evening constitutional, I was alarmed to observe a young lady, in considerable distress, supporting herself upon the railings of the pier. No doctor being readily at hand, I escorted the young woman to my rooms where she instantly gave birth to a child of the female sex. Though weak from her considerable exertions, the mother begged me to deliver the child into the hands of her sister and equipped me with your address for this purpose. Though happy to execute your sister's wishes I feel sure you will understand that I am not keen to be further involved. I have already in my charge an infant of the male sex who came to me through an equally unusual channel and his education alone has proved a great strain on my limited resources.

"I took the Christian precaution of having your niece baptized, lest she should not survive the arduous strain inflicted on all travellers by the Brighton Line. Happily though, the infant has lived through her ordeal; a testimony, I am sure, to the robust nature of the hand-bag in which you now find her. I named your niece 'Gwendolen' after the steam engine which bore her to London. I hope you approve of the epithet.
Yours sincerely, Mr Thomas James Cardew."

I surveyed the the letter once again but the charitable gentleman had failed to append an address. He did, however, provide a post script:

"PS I am sorry to report that your sister died soon after the birth. What shall I do with the body?"

Silence. Lady Bracknell is quite motionless. She moves to the vase. She now smashes the vase with extraordinary force. Lady Bracknell is quite motionless. Silence

I have always found Fate strangely unpredictable. Fate has no respect for the proper hierarchy of life and it's influence is as likely to be found in the great affairs of state as in the thickening of custard. This wilful disregard for correct behaviour has made Fate quite unacceptable in all the better households of London. Indeed, Mary Farquhar tells me that the modern sciences are soon to eliminate Fate almost entirely from our domestic lives. I hope she is correct in her speculation. Had Fate been a less frequent visitor in my own history my experiences might have been radically different. Perhaps even happy.

A long silence

Mary Farquhar also informs me that my milliner, Edith, has lately developed theatrical inclinations of the severest kind and intends imminently to embark upon a stage career of her own. (*Pause*) I see little future in it.

Pause. She turns toward the morning-room

Mr Worthing? Mr Worthing! Uncrimp, sir, my daughter from that corrugated posture! I must speak to you at once on a matter of vital importance.

Lady Bracknell turns back into the hall

Lady Bracknell's confinement.

Tableau

CURTAIN

FURNITURE AND PROPERTY LIST

On stage: Chair or sofa
Pedestal
Vase of white lilies

LIGHTING PLOT

Single interior setting
No property fittings required

To open: Bring up general interior effect

No cues